AGAI ALL ODDS

First Published in Great Britain in 2008 by Charles Emeka.

A CIP catalogue record for this title is available from the British Library

Book Jacket Design & Layout by:
www.byjomedia.com

ISBN 978-0-9561119-0-6
Typeset in Tahoma by Charles Emeka
Charles Emeka International
70 Nicholl House,
Spring Park Drive,
London N4 2TQ
www.charlesemeka.com
Printed and bound in the UK

Praise For Against All Odds

'Against all Odds is an inspiring and empowering book, that encourages readers to understand that our end can be better than our beginning, and that it is not how you start life, but how you finish. I hope this book inspires readers to overcome challenges and be the very best that they can be.'
Alison George

In teaching the importance of values and personal responsibility, Charles Emeka is making a positive and much-needed contribution to the ongoing discussion about youth crime.
Joseph Harker- The Guardian

As a child Charles Emeka gave Adults an opportunity to help him, they failed, As a teen Charles Emeka gave his friends an opportunity to help him, he was jailed, As a man Charles Emeka was given an opportunity to help himself he sailed, and now Charles is giving you an opportunity to learn from his mistakes. Don't waste it.
PC Miriam Virgo- ***Thames Valley Police***

Against All Odds is a must read for all young people and is testament to the fact that the success comes from within and the choices you choose to make along the way.
Francoise Moore- ***Bexley Education Services***

A tribute to Charles for taking the time to reach out to others through actions and words; let us pay tribute, in advance, to those who will take the time to benefit from his wise words, take action themselves and elevate
their lives into positive reality.
Verna Rhodes- ***Aspire Ambassador Coordinator***

Against All Odds - Essential and inspirational reading in these challenging times
Tony Nwachukwu- ***Founder of Burnt Progress & NEPA Ventures/Music producer***

Written from the heart, it speaks to the heart. Against All Odds will prove a must-have for young people on their journey through life. I wish I'd had this sort of moral support when I was younger.
Al Brunker- ***Speakers Bank Borough Coordinator & Associate Trainer***

FOREWORD BY NIMS OBUNGE. MBE

This heart-wrenching story awakens scenes from a challenging past. It is a story that demands our attention and brings hope to the most troubled soul. It also enables those who feel they have come to the end of the road see a way out. In this book, Charles has shared his life experience with unparalleled openness and vulnerability.

Charles Emeka's life is not merely that of a man whose dyslexia, sexual abuse and bullying led to a lifestyle of criminality and subsequent incarceration, but is also a story of triumph and remarkable transformation. Charles shares the practical secrets that make impossible situations possible. He highlights his struggles with gangs, guns and drugs, his encounter with God that led to a new life. His eleven candid and simple practical steps to turn one's life around are very easy to follow.

I often go into prisons demonstrating with a new crisp twenty-pound note that even after it has been crumpled, thrown to the ground and stamped on, its value is in no way diminished. This book is a strong reinforcement of this belief.

Often in life, events may not turn out as one anticipates but having gone from the pit of despair and degradation to prison, Charles has certainly commenced his journey to the palace of his dreams. He proves that you can achieve your dreams if only you are willing to pay the price.

'Against All Odds' is a must read for those who struggle with hope and those whose dream it is to bring change where it is most needed.

Nims Obunge
Chief Executive of The Peace Alliance

CONTENTS:

In Loving Memory of:

My father Julius O.A. Njoku (1932-2007) who passed away half way through me writing this book.
Dad, I pray God can give you a sneak preview of what I have been able to achieve and I just hope that in some little way, you were proud.
I wish you were still here so we could settle some scores, but God knows best.
You left as you wanted to, so I cannot really complain. You birthed my love for reading and writing; I know you wanted me to be a lawyer like you and to speak for the oppressed. I know you were disappointed when I chose a different path,
but I am sure you took some consolation in the fact that I ended up speaking, not in a court room but in schools, prisons and in conferences where people are emotionally, mentally, spiritually, relationally and financially oppressed.

May your soul rest in perfect peace. We miss you.

My cousin Andrew Nwachukwu, (1971-2003) the only reason why I do what I do. His death ushered me into a speaking career that I had not planned or dreamed of. I was asked to be the MC at his funeral. I gave a speech in which I was told by several people that I was born to speak for a living. I have never stopped speaking ever since.

Andrew, Sickle cell did not take you, you had finished your race and had spread your message of peace and love to all who needed to hear it. Andrew was the Retail Territory Manager for the Guardian and Observer newspapers for South London. A young man with wide interests - photography, the theatre and music among them;he was also on the committee of the Sickle Cell Society. His 1999 poem 'Sickle Cell Means', posted on the society's website, showed a positive approach he took to both his condition and his life. His sudden death leaves a gap that will be impossible to fill.

10% of every book sold will go towards the support of those dealing with Sickle Cell. For more information on Sickle Cell please visit www.sicklecellsociety.org or www.sicklecelldisease.org

Acknowledgements

Wow! This project actually came to pass. I am grateful to God for life, guidance, protection, direction, boldness and the courage to finish what I started, even when at times it seemed like a good idea to walk away and shut my mouth.
Many people would have been happy if I chose to do that, but it's not about those who are unduly worried about their reputation and image.

I am grateful to my family for putting up with me during trying times. We have not always seen eye to eye on numerous occasions, we have misunderstood each other at times, but I hope when all is said and done, you can somehow be proud of what I have achieved.

To my Pastor and God's mouth piece, Pastor Matthew Ashimolowo, may God continue to use you to speak to the nations and may he continue to give you wisdom, strength and direction as you continue to assist in releasing my potential and of all members of the Kingsway family. Thank you sir, I appreciate you.

To all members of the Kingsway family, thank you for all your support, encouragement and prayers.

Atiti Sosimi of Distinctly Different, you are the reason that this book was born. This was not my idea, but yours. You pushed me when I did not want to move. I remember sitting in your office when you told me to write a short essay on my life. What was meant to be an essay of a few pages has now become this book. I went through so many emotions as pen met with paper. At times I resented you and thought you were being tough on me. But I knew you always had my best interests at heart. I appreciate all you have done for me and my story will never be complete without your input. By having you as a mentor is like having a secret weapon in my corner.

Richie Dayo Johnson, of Richmond Johnson Academy, you opened my eyes to what was truly possible. You embraced me when I was unknown. You always answered my calls even when it was not convenient and you have helped to open doors that may have been harder to open without your influence and endorsement. I was guaranteed to succeed once you became my mentor.

Ore Ogunbayi of Speakers Bank and Toastmasters International, I thank you for trusting and giving me my first paid speaking job. You have continued to bring opportunities my way, put money in my pocket and have continued to be a source of encouragement and support.

Caroline Clark, regional co-coordinator Speakers Bank, you spoke up and stood up for me when I could no longer speak for myself and you have continued to present me with training and speaking opportunities. Thank you for trusting me with the ears and minds of young people in your boroughs.

Justin Smith, my boss at Youth Media, if you had not taken me for lunch, fired me and then given me £1,000.00 to start my own business, I may not be here now. Thank you for all the continuous advice and encouragement and for being a role model worth emulating.

Kimberlie Andrew of the BBC, you took this book to another level when you put your flavour into it. You are great at what you do and I am sure it is only a matter of time before we see your book on the shelves of book stores. You were born to write and to make a difference. I am grateful for the time you gave to this book and also the speed in which you did it. Thank you does not really shine light on my true appreciation.

Ann Mark, my wonderful cousin. You have been there from the beginning in good times and in bad. You have covered me even when I have caused you embarrassment and grief. No matter how many times I messed up, you still had something extra to give to me. You edited this book when it was still in my hand writing on paper and gave me the belief to go on. I love you.

Eugenia Aidoo, you took time out of your busy schedule to check this book for errors on at least three occasions. Your encouragement in those moments when I was weak and fatigued made the difference. Akira and Akina, thank you for all the prayers and songs of support and encouragement. I will never forget "He knows my name". I have no doubt that the two of you will grow up to be women of standard and I believe you will stay on course and fulfill your potential.

Dr Ogo Eze, London's finest Dentist, you have been focused on seeing me win in life. You refuse to let me rest on my laurels, you have stood with me when you could have taken easier options. You have kept me posted on relevant information on a weekly basis. You have kept my teeth in the best condition possible to keep speaking and smiling and you have continued to make sure that I brush my teeth twice a day. I appreciate you for all you do and have done for me. I'm grateful.

To my friend, product/graphic designer Joe Ademosu (www.byjomedia.com), a lot of friends come and go, but you are truly a friend for life. You are gifted and it's only a matter of time before your designs are seen all over the world. I love you man.

To all my colleagues at Speakers Bank and Toastmasters International, may we continue to speak up speak out and remain voices of hope.

All the members of the ICSN family, I know some of the contents of this book will shock you but I hope you enjoy the read all the same. Thank you for the opportunity to lead you guys and I am sure the best is still set to come.

To every young person who has sat down or stood up and allowed me to speak before them without throwing tomatoes at me or booing me off stage, to every attendee or delegate that has attended any seminar or conference where I have spoken, thank you for your time.

To the entire design team at Splash of London, you are truly a quality media solutions company. You always make the difference.

My appreciation goes out to my cousins, Stephanie for typing the manuscript, Frank for designing the second illustration for the book and Tracey for proof reading and editing the book before print.

My Story

Within hours of me being born I was dead. Yes that's what I said, DEAD. That should have been an early indication for me that life wasn't going to be an easy ride. I'm Charles by the way, from Hackney. Nice to meet you. Apparently because I was born premature I needed some extra medication to help me out. The only problem with that was the nurses injected me with the wrong medication and well, I died they said.
Obviously they saved me which is why you are able to read my book, but there have been a few times when I wished they hadn't bothered.

I lived in Hackney with my mum, dad and my older brother Leo. I know people think Hackney is really bad and, okay, there are a couple of stabbings, robberies and murders daily; BUT it wasn't that bad when I was growing up. In fact it was cool and there was a real sense of community. Things started to take a downward turn when I started primary school.

I don't know why but reading and writing wasn't really my thing. Don't get me wrong, I tried but it just wasn't working for me. So I was seen as well… a bit thick. Everyone else was normal and getting on with things and I felt like the stupid, odd one out. The teachers thought I was a waste of space and told my parents as much. My father refused to accept that and made sure I got some extra help with a tutor for development and to understand why I just wasn't getting it in class. I was later diagnosed as having severe dyslexia. Basically, I struggled with letters on the page and muddled them up. Finally there was a reason why it was so difficult for me. I should have felt great that I was not a nut job, but I didn't really, it left me a bit sad.

I had to work harder than most because words were difficult for me to comprehend. I was given a learning mentor – yeah I had never heard of one of them either until I needed one – and she was patient with me and I became the best reader in the class within six months. Her name was Mrs Cronk. Did life get better? Nope my confidence was shot. I think I might have hated myself a little and if I didn't then what followed definitely convinced me.

When I was nine something really horrible happened to me. It's still difficult to talk about it now, way over twenty years later. A woman from my estate decided that she was going to do some not-so-nice things to me. She took me to a derelict building on the estate. I had always been scared of that place. It was a cold building, all grey and looked really lonely. There was no one there and she sexually abused me. I didn't know how to feel, where to go and what to say. I went home and as a child never told a soul.

The incident left me feeling numb and very much confused. As I couldn't tell anyone it just played on my mind over and over again. I felt embarrassed and ashamed. Mentally, it crippled me and emotionally I was all over the place and I withdrew from my friends and family. I know I should have told someone, but who? And how do you even begin to say out the words? If it was you, who would you have told?

Because I pulled myself away from normal things and reality, I am sure my friends must have thought I was going mad. They started to make fun of me and later it would become bullying. My family had no idea what was going on in my head and although they were concerned, they couldn't understand why I had changed from my normal self to this quiet withdrawn child.

Throughout my school life I was bullied more or less everyday. I was the local joke, everyone and anyone had a pop. I felt like nothing, like no one, I was by myself and no one seemed to care.

One day I watched one of the Rocky films and it really had an impact on me. I decided enough was enough, if he could do it, so could I. Even as the underdog he worked his way up and became the champion. I didn't want to be a champion I just wanted people to stop taking the piss. I watched the rest of the Rocky films and they became great motivators. They made me believe in myself and I knew from then on that I would never be bullied again.
So I am at school, minding my own business and one of my regular tormentors decide that I was his choice of ridicule and embarrassment for

the day. Ordinarily I would just let it happen and pray he'd get bored and move on. But on this particular day, something snapped and I decided to fight back.

I kicked, punched and fought with everything I had. I really thought I had got to the point of no return and I didn't care if he killed me, but I had to give it my all. And then it happened. Usually, when being bullied, in my head I would be saying 'please stop', so you can imagine my shock when my bully started begging me to stop. I couldn't bloody believe it. This thug that made it his job to punish me daily and make my life a misery was begging me for mercy, I would have laughed if it wasn't so weird. And then to top things off all the other kids started cheering me on. I was the MAN.

I mean, I was really the man and it felt brilliant. For the first time other kids saw me, not as a doormat, but as someone to be reckoned with. I can't explain to you how that made me feel. Special doesn't begin to touch it. So I did what any kid with a new found strength would do, I continued to batter him with all my new Rocky punches.

It was a new day, I felt so elated that if I could have slowly smoked a fag like those cool gangsters on the TV did after a battle, I would have. Problem was of course, I was a kid and didn't know how to smoke, but you get my drift. From that moment onwards, I was never bullied again.

In fact to some of the kids I was a bit like a mini hero. I had lots of new friends and the fame to go with it because I had knocked the school bully off his throne. The news quickly spread around the whole school and to neighbouring schools. Things seemed to be much better for me.

However, with my fame came another problem, one I hadn't bargained for. The more I grew in popularity, the more I realised I had morphed into a bully. I'm not sure at what point it happened, but I know that I had no respect for my family or authority. I terrorized the neighbourhood. I did what I wanted, when I wanted and I demanded respect. Imagine that! I demanded respect. I didn't know then that you will only get true respect through honest means, but for me, respect was all I wanted by any means necessary. The more I fought and won the more respect I got. I had this sense of amazing power that now went with me and my prolific reputation.

Even though I was receiving the respect I had always craved, I was still really angry and I didn't know why. Everything seemed cool but even when I had a brilliant day it just didn't feel complete and I wasn't sure where my life was going. Don't worry this isn't the part where I tell you I found Jesus and accepted him as my lord and saviour, you wouldn't believe me anyway.

Things started to spiral out of control, way out of control. My fights became more vicious and I started shoplifting, hot wiring cars, stealing from the cars, putting petrol bombs through letter boxes. Robbing and mugging old people became the norm for me. It didn't affect me. I felt nothing. I did not feel bad about it, just okay actually. But when you start to get a bit out of control you want more and more. That's why people who start drinking can easily become alcoholics and why people can move from a bit of weed to crack cocaine in next to no time at all.
That is exactly what happened to me. First I just wanted to experiment, why not? I could do what I wanted, when I wanted and no one could tell me anything. So I tried out some cannabis to find out what it was all about. It was okay, but I wanted something more. I then went on to much more powerful drugs. I hated it, but continued taking drugs just to be popular. You see my peers expected me to take it, that's what Charles does, 'he does what he wants, and he's not scared'. I was cool. Looking back now, I realise I was a cool fool.
When the drugs had worn off, why was I so confused?
How come I didn't know if I was coming or going? And how come that feeling always came back after the drugs wore off?

By the time I was 18, all my friends were drug users and I became a bit of an expert on various drugs, if I do say so myself. My drugs partner in crime became alcohol; they were as close as the rapper 50 Cent and his bullet proof vest. And for me the combination was lethal and the effect menacing. Rage, my goodness, rage! I had such outbursts of anger that I have no idea where they came from or how I eventually calmed down.

This was common for all my friends too.

The gang was now involved in drug dealing, just saying no was not an option for us. Did we know that drugs could kill people? YES. Did we care? NO. It was every man for himself. If you decided you wanted to take drugs, it was not my job to judge. Knock yourself out.

Drugs and violence started to become a given and we needed to do some other things to keep us going. Then the new craze was born, less work, more money - fraud and deception. It became massive in the 90's. It was all the rage, taking people's money without their consent. Ingenious! Once we mastered our formula and put a system in place, it worked daily like clock work and life, to be quite frank, was brilliant.

Out of that, my relationship with the police was born. I was always getting arrested. In fact, I got arrested so much I knew that by law, if the police asked to search me, I could in turn ask to search them first. People being planted with drugswas common. Honestly it's the absolute truth. I would say try it if you don't believe me but it's probably not a good idea. It never went down too well but it did give me a couple of laughs searching them when I informed them of my rights while they read me mine. Every time they arrested me, they never seemed to have enough evidence to prosecute me.

Most of my offences led to cautions, fines and community service. Community service, what was that about? An opportunity to spend days at a time with other criminals, great idea law makers, it is definitely the best way to get me to turn my life around, duh!

So I began to think I was invincible and untouchable. I was the one they could not catch. For long periods of time, they just couldn't get me. Either I was really brilliant or the authorities were rubbish or didn't care. Drug dealing remained our bread and butter, it didn't matter what else we got into, we always knew we could count on people's addiction to drugs to line our pockets. We were always on hand to help people feed their destructive habits.

Being involved in this kind of lifestyle meant, at some stage, you would have to get to the point of no return. Face the barrel of a gun or the blade of a knife. It comes with the territory. People were always trying to see how far they could go with you, or trying to get a piece of the action. So drug dealing always had to be backed up with violence so that one could maintain respect and territory.

In the year 2000, I was involved in a stabbing incident in a club (Leisure Lounge) in the west end of London. I say involved, but I may have even caused it. Who knows? All I do know is events following it led to the beginning of the end. A massive fight had broken out between my crew and another crew. I can't even remember their name but it was mortal combat on a different level. Looking back it reminds me of fighting games on Nintendo you know, like it didn't exist, make believe. Things happened so fast and it was over before you could blink. The club was covered in broken glass, I mean it was everywhere. People in the club all ran for the exit at the same time which caused a stampede and chaos. People got crushed and injured in the process.

My cousin was repeatedly stabbed in his chest and in his back. It was the first time a blood relative had been hit in front of my own eyes. He was lying on the floor saturated in blood, shaking. I made sure someone called an ambulance and I tried to reassure him that he was going to be fine, just a war wound. I took off my jacket to cover the wounds that wouldn't stop pouring blood. My cousin told me he couldn't feel his legs and he was really cold. He thought he was dying. He was convinced it was his time to check out and asked me to promise him his pregnant girlfriend and unborn child would be looked after. It was the first time I considered my own mortality. I was in this same altercation but did not have a single scratch on me. Against all odds, my life had been spared for another day.

That same year I started to receive death threats. People don't like to see you become "successful", if you want to call it that. They all want a piece of the action and many are willing to do almost anything to get it. It was no biggy, things like this are expected when you choose to live above the law. Call it an occupational hazard. If you choose to live by violence, there is a high chance that violence will also cut your life short. I'm sure you have heard the saying, 'Live by the sword, die by the sword.'

My first real brush with the sword came shortly after. The gang and I were traveling en mass to a private house party. We went because we wanted to have a good time, but of course, we were always prepared for it to kick off at any moment. As I said before, just a bit of an occupational hazard. An hour into the party, we were embroiled in a severe altercation with a rival gang. All hell had broken loose. Various weapons were on display and there seemed to be broken bottles everywhere as usual.

The drama spilled onto the streets. A few people were injured, but my crew were untouched, because that's how we rolled, mercenaries. The police arrived and things ended abruptly and the rival gang fled for safety. The cowards. We went back inside and celebrated our victory, we never ran, always faced the beef, that meant something to me. Our celebration was short lived, the rival gang returned with back up and new recruits. They made their way back into the house without anyone really taking note of them. I was standing with my back to the stairs and before I knew what was going on, a gun was placed firmly on my stomach.

I spun around to face my accomplice and realised what was going on. Immediately, probably for the first time in a long time, I was petrified. All of a sudden it was silent. I don't know if it was just in my head or if the whole house was in fact in silence. People appeared to be staring, and it seemed as though people were holding their breath collectively. From the corner of my eye, I could see my brother, gripped with fear, tears rolling down his face. I knew that was it, the point of no return.

Without thinking about it, I shouted at the gunman to pull the trigger. I was angry, scared, lost, vulnerable. I felt exactly how I felt when I was bullied. But I knew never again, never again would I be showing fear ever again, I'll never be bullied ever again. "PULL THE TRIGGER, PULL IT, PULL IT!" I shouted. Everyone waited for the gun to go off. Everyone was waiting for my body to freeze on the impact of the bullet and then slowly slump to the ground signifying the end of my life. I maintained eye contact with my accomplice. I was not happy with my life. I had contemplated suicide on a few occasions, so to have someone take my life was ideal at the time. Nothing happened.

"For some reason I just can't shoot you" the gun man said, "I've done it before, I should be able to do it again!". And he walked away with his gang following him. Just like that.

My next flash with death came two weeks later when I was involved in a car crash. I was drunk and was speeding home when my car crashed on the A13 motorway right next to the Blackwall Tunnel in East London. I should have been dead, but I crawled away with only minor injuries. That happened to be on a Sunday evening and I was so frightened and thankful I was alive that I went to church for the first time in a real long time.

I have to be honest and say going to church for me wasn't strictly a result of my concern over my mortality, some of my associates had told me that there were so many girls there and the church preached sermons that were useful in everyday life. So I figured I could kill two birds with one stone.

I really needed help but I was too arrogant to admit it, so my focus at the church was going to be the girls. When I arrived that evening at the church, the man at the pulpit (Pastor Matthew) was saying "if what you have been doing is not working for you, don't you think it's time to try something else. Drink and drugs will not heal your pain, anger, violence and rebellion to authority will get you nowhere. You were born a ten, don't die a three."

Oh Lord! I found myself crying. I mean crying like never before. I found it all so overwhelming. For the whole service, I just cried and realised how many close shaves I had had with death. I knew it was time to throw in the towel just as Rocky did when he accomplished his dreams. I knew if I continued with my lifestyle someone would kill me or I would end up in prison, but I had no idea how to change or even where to start. In that

game you didn't just decide 'oh well, that's me done, it's a wrap!' There are consequences for that sort of weakness. That's exactly what it would be seen as - weakness.
Having thought about it, I went back to my trusted friend, alcohol, it never let me down. I couldn't be seen to be going soft. I had a so-called reputation to uphold and I couldn't be seen to be letting my guard down or anything. No way, no how! So I rid my mind of doing better by drinking like it was going out of fashion.

Two days later, I had another court appearance. Nothing new really, it was at Marylebone Magistrates Court. It was no big deal. I figured I'd be in and out in a couple of hours max. Been there, done that! I was right; the court proceedings went very quickly. After all deliberations the judge asked me to stand. I stood up, a cocky smirk on my face, I had been at this juncture many times before. I could do with a bit of community service actually, catch up with a couple of old associates and see what's good. "You continue to be a menace to society and today you will know that you are truly not above the law, you are going to prison", he pronounced.

I was informed that I had been found guilty which was no surprise to me and I was being sent to Wandsworth Prison in South London. Just like that. No discussion, no negotiations, no deal brokering just like that, deal done. For the first time in a long time I could see clearly. I didn't want to cry, but even my tears sold out on me and they were streaming down my face. This wasn't what I wanted. I was scared for real and I had no one to blame but myself. The show was over, the game was up. The gang was nowhere to be seen. Where were they now that I needed them? There was no dope to smoke and no crack to sell. There was no alcohol to numb the pain and blur the reality of life. I was now on my own to pay the full price for all my actions. I pinched myself hoping it was just a bad dream.

Prison is like another planet. Nothing on the outside has any meaning or relevance. I wasn't Charles anymore I was FR4436. Nobody cares who you are, they are too busy having their own pity party or pretending they don't need one. Feelings don't count for much. There are no dinner menu's to choose from. You are given permission to walk, eat, talk, sleep

and think. Imagine that, permission.
If you do the crime, you will eventually do the time. I was the son of a lawyer about to go on a long vacation to one of Her Majesty's prisons to hang out with murderers, armed robbers, rapists, paedophiles and various degrees of criminals. The hardest thing for me was acknowledging I was one of them.

There are two types of pain in life, the pain of discipline and the pain of regret. I immediately began to experience the pain of regret, as I was led away to begin serving my sentence. In the prison system, your family background, class, race, upbringing and education count for nothing. You are nothing more than a number and that's it.

If I had realised this was going to happen, I would have made sure I had a good meal before coming to court because it was going to be my last decent one for awhile. If I had known I would have told my family that I was sorry and I loved them because I now would not be able to tell them for a long time. If I had just an inclination, I would have prayed to God to help me change rather than hoping that twenty-three hours locked up in a cell would change me.

If I could have, I would have got help while I was free. The only help available to me inside was a key that opened the door but it was the same key that locked me back in. My home was now a place where I was caged in by bricks, concrete and steel.

If I thought I had felt lonely before in life, it was nothing compared to prison. Nothing. I'm not afraid to admit, I struggled to cope in prison daily. And so does everyone. Don't believe anyone who says it doesn't affect them, because all that means is it affected them so badly they have blocked out the reality. The mental and emotional pressure you feel you are under when locked in a thirteen foot room is overwhelming. I understand why people kill themselves and lose it in prison. Trying to keep it together is hard and at times, I thought I had got to my point of no return but against all odds, I kept on going.

Things became a little better when the toughest guy in the prison gave me a Bible. He was doing a fifteen-year sentence and he had been in and out of prison from a very early age. His name was Steve and for some reason he had my back. Steve was an armed robber and professional criminal who could push a hundred press-ups on his knuckles without losing his breath. When you have all that time on your hands, you tend to spend it building muscle and power because you are never sure when you are going to need it.

I'll never forget the day he looked at me and said "You don't want this life, it leads to nowhere but downward. Prison life will make you hate like you have never hated before, it will make you hurt like you have never hurt before and it will destroy you mentally, emotionally and psychologically. When you get out of here, don't you dare come back. If you come for a second stretch, know you will be coming here for the rest of your life."

He was right. Prison is not a joke, it's not a game on PlayStation or Xbox and it's not a movie in Hollywood. It's real. I had to lose my freedom to appreciate it. Prison magnifies your emotions, if you are unhappy now, you will be screwed in prison. It will destroy your soul, your mind and your spirit if you are weak. If it's bullies you are hiding from, they are all in there waiting to welcome you. You see, people try to not focus on themselves in prison so they do anything to break up the day with that hour of association they have. The sorts of people who thrive on being locked away from other humans for 23 hours are genius types, scientists who enjoy questioning life's big questions. If that's not you, oh well. And it wasn't me.

Prison life will debase your mind. In prison, you will go through every mental and emotional feeling that exists. It is not something that is easy to get used to. To have an appreciation of prison life, lock yourself up in your bedroom for a week. Close your curtains, don't look out the window, switch off your mobile phone, pull out the landline from the socket, keep a bucket in your room for a toilet, forget about showers and baths and you will start to get a fraction of the idea. I am telling you, you don't

want this. I have never met anyone in prison who did want this.
The food you eat is cooked by prisoners. God help you if you are sharing a cell with someone. I did. He was a heroine addict, who now had no access to drugs and you could see him losing his marbles and deteriorating with each passing day. That same cell where you eat and sleep is the same cell where you must use the toilet with no demarcations. I hope you get the picture.

While in Prison, I saw lots of young people on antidepressants and other forms of medication. There were others on twenty-four hour watch. People attempting suicide was normal and some inmates succeeded in checking out early from life.

One night there was non-stop screaming through the night. I just wanted it to stop. It was just a constant shrill and I wanted to sleep and not think about it or where I was. It was horrible, really horrible. When whoever it was eventually stopped screaming, I was so relieved. It's not nice being awake at night in prison. The silence comforted me from the screams of desperation. The next day I found out the reason the noise stopped was because that man had killed himself. The silence now was deafening. I would never feel the same again. You always knew when someone had killed themselves. The atmosphere would change. Prison has the ability to turn a real bad boy from the street into a timid, fearful, psychological wreck. These are people just like you and I.

Society is so messed up that going to prison gives you bragging rights. People have send-offs and homecoming parties. This really is not a life you would want. Being caged in, being locked up, being put out of normal society and human circulation is not honourable or smart. You don't have to learn the way I did, the hard way. Take my word for it. Was I a vicious raping, murdering beast? No, but I was in the same house as them. Did I play sexually with children? No, but I lived with paedophiles and other sick and psychotic individuals.

The Bible became my staple. It broke up the twenty-three hours a day. The more I read it, the more questions it answered for me and the more my thinking started to shift. I knew I could not come out of prison to continue my gang activities. I couldn't go back to violence. I learnt that it wasn't in my heart, it wasn't what I felt. I recognised that drug dealing, fraud and deception would no longer cut it. If things were going to change, I had to decide to change while still caged up. It was now or never. I had another lifeline and it may have been the last one. I had had so many, but there was no guarantee that I would have any more.

Today, life is much better for me, but if you put that number code into any prison system, my name would still come up. A very real reminder of a past I would prefer to forget. You don't need that sort of reminder. Let my reminder serve as yours. I know one of the hardest things out there these days is peer pressure. You want to belong, be understood and be down. A gang offers you some sense of security and family, right? They will ride or die for you, right? Well those words are used to create a false sense of comfort. For every young person that decides to walk down this route and be down, here is what is guaranteed: death or getting locked up.

When I speak to drug dealers, peddlers, hustlers as they like to be called, and ask them what would make them stop living this way, they generally all have the same answer, "I will stop when I have made enough money, I will start my own business, buy my own house, provide for my family, have the things I want and get out of the game". But catch this, I have never met a dealer that retired of his own free will. I have never heard anyone say "I have made enough money now and I'm done". They all come into early retirement because they met with the blade of a knife, a bullet from a gun or the steel and iron of walls of a prison.

I have experienced the loss of loved ones, and I'm sure if they could come back for five minutes, the one thing they would all say is 'Do not live your life as if you have a spare one'. I know it sounds airy fairy but it's only through education, developing yourself personally, choosing to win the right way in life and surrounding yourself with positive people that you will earn the money you need and live the life you want. The more you learn, the more you earn. Remember, readers are leaders.

If you don't hear anything else I have said, then catch this. Without meeting you, without knowing your story, I do know this: within you lies the seeds of greatness. You have potential, you have gifts and you have talents, don't take them to the grave. Let your life mean something and be worth something. You don't have to just pass through life aimlessly, you can make an impact if you want to.

Although we have come to the end of a chapter in this book, you can make this the first chapter in your life. On the pages that follow I have added what was for me the tool kit which helped me turn my life around after prison and have purpose. Part of that purpose is to help inspire people who believe they are worth more, to be more. You can turn any mess into a message that will empower someone else. You must be willing to sacrifice to achieve. I am sorry if like me, you have had to experience certain things that you probably didn't have to. The truth is bad things happen to good people. But you can still make it. Get up and shake off the mistakes of the past. If you don't let go of your past, you can't take hold of your future. It's not too late, come back from your point of no return. You are a survivor and you were born to win. See you at the top because it's crowded at the bottom.

Pen Time
Part 1

1. Make a list of bad things that have happened to you.

2. List past mistakes you have made.

....
....
....
....
....
....
....
....
....
....
....
....
....
....
....
....
....
....
....
....
....
....
....
....
....
....
....
....
....
....
....

3. What parts of your life are holding you back from fulfilling your potential.

4. List negative/draining people around you that you need to keep at a distance.

5. What areas in your life do you still have struggles with.

IN & OUT

STEPS TO GETTING OUT & STAYING OUT OF TROUBLE

CHARLES EMEKA

Maybe you have just read my story and want to change your life or you are looking for some quick life skills to get you on your way, either way, welcome. This is a comprehensive guide for people who have had to deal with trouble or are themselves in a bit trouble. Let me firstly say, this is the beginning of the rest of your life. We can't rewrite your history but we can prepare for your future and help you to make better informed choices. Trouble is a state or a cause of distress, pain, inconvenience, fear or confusion.

Peer pressure exists. You are not going mad, you are not weak, it exists and always has done. But guess what, I've got your back. Maybe you are part of a gang and considering life on the other side, I know it seems an impossible dream but please hang with me for a little while. Maybe like the old me, experimenting with drugs or selling it is your thing. I just want this book to help you consider your options. If you are binge drinking, have unexplained aggression, not sure what the future holds, caught in between two mindsets, scared or frustrated, then please stay with me for a little while.

Are you truanting from school? Then hold it for a moment. Lend me your eyes and your ears. Are you a young person involved in random, casual sex? Are you always up for a fight? Do you lose your temper easily? Do you go into a rage without thinking twice? Then we do have a lot in common.

Whatever the situation or scenario, if you're at a place and you don't know the next step to take, I believe you have picked up the right book at the right time and I hope, by the right author. I hope I have got something for you. It might just be a piece of the pie, but then you have one less piece to get. That in itself is progress.

Wherever you are in your life, whatever trouble you may already be in or could be getting into, it's not too late to turn things around. How do I know? I am glad you asked. I know because I was probably in a worse position or in the same conditions that you are in right now. Everything I mentioned previously was me not so long ago. I am not talking ten or twenty years ago. I am talking a little while ago. A few years back. I always used to be in trouble. I was in trouble with my family, the police, the authorities, gangs, people and myself. Where I was, trouble was. That's just the way it was. I was highly influenced by peer pressure. I used to be in a gang. I used to take drugs and sell drugs. I used to drink large amounts of alcohol in quick succession. I was bullied and then I became a bully. I did not like school very much and wondered what the point was. For me school was a necessary evil. I was involved in a lot of casual sex and as I got older, I eventually paid the price for my actions. With the life I lived, outbursts of anger and violence came with it. So as you can see, I am qualified to talk about trouble but my focus is that you get out of it for good.

Trouble is something that generally moves in a downward spiral. Whatever your trouble is right now, today is a good day to start dealing with it. Now is the time to say enough is enough.

Look, I know your reason for being in trouble or getting into trouble may not have initially been your fault. But if you choose to remain in the trouble, you will have to accept that you made those decisions. That may sound harsh, but I am not writing this book to hype you up, I am writing it to help you.

It really is crowded at the bottom and there is so much room for you at the top, so may I suggest that you 'walk this way'. Irrespective of how long you have been in your present predicament, things can turn around very quickly. May I use this opportunity to plead with you; do not live your life as if you have a spare one. You owe it to yourself to give life your best shot. You owe it to yourself to be the best you can be.

As young people, we want to be liked and we want to be popular. The problem is some of us would rather be popular than be bright. Popularity can be a good thing, if it is for the right reasons. Let us choose not to major in minor things.

Cause & Effect
For every action, there is a reaction. That's a principle of life that cannot be altered, not even for you. There is a price to pay for everything you do. May I go further to say that nothing in life is free? For every motion or action you embark on there will surely be an outcome.

Here is something else I need you to consider, you have a choice in the action but your say in the reaction is limited. Let me give you an example. I may decide that going to school is not cool. I may convince myself that school is for weak people, boffins and nerds. So not going to school is my action but here comes the reaction.

No school equals no qualifications or poor grades. No qualifications generally mean a higher chance of unemployment or unskilled work, which in turn means minimum wage or a poor salary. Having minimal income means next to no buying power, which will of course affect how you live the rest of your life. And really, that's just for starters. I could go into living conditions, health and lifestyle. The list is endless.

I hear you saying that you are still young. You won't be young forever and life has a way of catching up with you. I am sure you get where I am coming from.

I am not saying that everyone has to go to university but I am saying, whatever level you are at right now you should be giving it your all. Even if for some reason you don't make it, at least you can say you gave it your best shot. And your best is good enough no matter the outcome.

Now to round up this point, a poor education can become a major limitation in your life. Why would you want to limit yourself? I am sure you don't. If you have an opportunity to get a good education, please do not waste it. There are many young people all over the world that would happily take your seat.

Let me appeal to you, if you are supposed to be in school and you're not, then you are damaging your own future and destiny. I am telling you this from personal experience. My not attending school regularly at times has been a handicap for me in many ways.

Bad Things Happen To Good People

Now I hear you saying, 'You don't understand where I am coming from. You don't know what I've been through. You can't relate to my situation. I did nothing wrong. I was an innocent child caught up in my parents' problems. I have had a hard start to life. Some adults took advantage of me. I don't know who my dad is. My mum went to the shops one day and never came back. The woman I have called mum is actually my grandmother and the woman I call auntie or sister is actually my mum. My dad has been in prison since I was young. My mum is hooked on crack cocaine or heroin. My parents told me they wish I was never born. My mum told me I was a mistake. One of my parents committed suicide. I find it hard to read or even do basic maths and the kids in school laugh at me. I was bullied. My parents could not afford for me to have the latest clothes and I was always being made fun of. I've been told I'm too fat'.

The list is endless. These statements are the reality of so many young people, maybe even you. These are common feelings and emotions that young people all over the world experience daily. Sometimes adults fail to stop and realise that this young person or that young person may have been exposed to horrible things and real negative experiences.

If this, young friend, is your story or something you encountered, I just want to say I am truly sorry that you had to experience that or hear such horrible things. Nobody should have to go through that. The crux of the matter, however, is that people do every day. Sometimes, life will throw some hard punches at you, even when you are young. You hear the statement all the time, 'that's life!' There are many things that happen in our lives that do not seem fair or justifiable especially when we are young. Being sexually abused at nine was not fair, being stereotyped by teachers was not fair and being bullied at school was wrong and hard to swallow. But I will say this, all those experiences have made me the man I am today.

As young people, we must have the ability to roll with those punches that do not feel fair at the time when they are thrown. Yes, you may have been knocked down but you must refuse to be knocked out. You must get back up again. Shake off the blow and fight one more round.

If you have got this book in your hand and you have read this far, you have already come along way. You are a survivor and I salute you. So, you can't give up now. If someone has hurt you and you now decide to give up, then you have let that person win and that is too much power for you to give to someone else. The things you have been through and experienced are just a chapter in your story. I believe your final chapter will make a wonderful ending. Trust me, it's not over yet.

Let me share a few things with you. There is nothing great, honourable or glorifying about being locked up in a cell. Having a baby when you are not ready for one is not an achievement. Stealing from people does not make you smart. Beating other people up does not make you strong. Shooting someone does not make you a soldier. Bullying other people should never make you feel better about yourself. Pointing out other people's weaknesses and flaws does not make you better than them. Taking drugs and binge drinking does not make you brave. Doing those things prove you don't have a lot of respect for yourself and you must question how much you value life and yourself.

Maybe you don't value who you are and that's an issue we will address in this section.
If you respect yourself then you will respect others, and if you respect yourself there are certain things you just won't do.

Who Are You?
Listen, just in case nobody has ever told you this, I hope you can believe me when I say, you have value. You are precious and important even if it does not feel like that right now. The world needs someone like you to be the best you can be. Do you know there is a particular thing that nobody on the face of the earth can do better than you? Six point two billion people on the face of the earth, and if you don't do that thing, nobody else

will. Nobody can ever be you better than you. They can try, but they are guaranteed to fail. People can try to dress like you, walk like you and talk like you, but they will never be you.

In the same way, you can never be anyone else but you. You were born an original, so don't die a photocopy. Why would you even want to be someone else? If two of us are the same, then one of us is unnecessary. The biggest issue with young people is that we are all trying to be like someone else. We try and dress like those we admire, we try and walk like those we respect. We buy things we can't afford to be like someone else. Ladies, we lose weight by whatever means to look like someone or to get other people's attention. Losing weight can be a good thing, but if you are going to do it, do it for you, do it for your health and for the right reasons.

As young men, we risk our lives and our futures just to be popular. When I went to prison, not one of my so-called friends came to visit or even ask how I was doing. The people I was trying to impress on a daily basis could not care less and had moved on once I was out of the picture.

Please be careful who you call your friends. You will only know who your true friends are when something happens or you go through something serious. For a relationship to be qualified as a friendship it needs a level of pressure applied to it. Things need to be a bit out of order for you to see how in order your so called friendship really is.

In this life you don't owe anyone anything apart from being the best you can be. While you are spending all your time and energy being someone else we never get to meet the real you. So you exist and pass through life without ever showing up. What a tragedy. Hear me when I say this and I say it all the time, 'people are entitled to have an opinion of you, but the only one that counts is the one you have of yourself'.

Some Questions

So let me ask you this, what do you think of yourself? Let me take it further, where is your life going? What vision, dreams and goals do you have for the future? If fear and failure did not exist, what would you love to be doing? I did not say like to do, I said love to do. You will only truly succeed in what you are passionate about. Who do you respect and admire? Who are your role models? If you could meet anyone in the world, who would it be and why? If you met them, what would you ask them?

I need you to consider these questions and ponder on them for a while. May be you could write down the answers in a special notebook.

Please do me a favour, do not give up on life so soon. Your parents' negative experiences do not have to be your reality. Your friends' problems don't have to be yours. Look around you. Look at your family, friends and associates. Look at those whose lifestyle you would not like to have and look at those who are going through trouble. That can't be what you want for your life. There has to be more for you than you're seeing right now. Now look at the lives of those you like and respect. That could be you, and that will be you with a few adjustments - some right decisions and positive action. There is so much more for you out there than what's happening in the area you live in right now.

Sometimes the media is quick to tell us all the negative things young people are doing. What about when these young people turn their lives around? How many people report on that? Who tells us about the positive things young people are doing? Maybe the media never will, because good news does not sell. But you can tell your own story just like I have started to tell mine. Nobody will ever be able to tell your story better than you. But for you to tell that story in your own words there is a price to pay.

You need to get out of trouble and stay out of trouble. You need to get right, get good and get going now. I have a speech titled 'If it's going to be, it's up to me'. There are certain things others can do for you but ultimately, it comes down to you and your decisions.
I challenge you right now to choose to win in life. I challenge you to be the best you can be. I challenge you to be you. So what's it going to be? Are you coming with me or are you going to sell yourself short?

I have said before that there are two types of pain, the pain of discipline and the pain of regret. The pain of discipline says you go through the following steps with me, implement them in your life and become the champion that you are.
The pain of regret says I ignore this joker, he's lived his life, now let me live mine. The pain of regret says I won't get caught, I won't get pregnant, I won't get stabbed, I won't get shot. The pain of regret says I don't need school, I'm going to make music, even though I have no qualifications. Do you know how many young people are trying to make music, become actors, singers or premiership footballers? We are talking millions every year. Before you disqualify me, all I am saying is that you need a back up plan. You need substitutes and additions to augment your ultimate goal. As a wise man once said, "write your dream in ink, but make your plans in pencil".
The pain of regret says I will take these drugs just one more time but, on this occasion, you don't come round from getting high and now we are planning a funeral. I'm sure you get the picture.

I hereby invite you to go through the steps coming up. They helped me, I'm sure they can help you. Now just in case you are still in doubt, remember my story that I let you in on earlier, where I discuss my former lifestyle in a little more detail? I was everything negative. My habits, attitude, actions and beliefs were all wrong. I terrorised neighbourhoods, I made people's lives a misery. In the end, I was given free boarding and lodging at one of Her Majesty's prisons.
Today, I'm proud to say that I am a speaker, Toastmaster, trainer, learning mentor and author. If I could change, then you definitely will change, if you want to.

Do you want to be just a meaningless statistic on a census report, or do you want to have a life in which you and those you love are truly productive and fulfilled?
So what's it going to be? It's your call, but if you get on these steps, your life will never be the same no matter how bad it looks right now. All you have to do is take the first step.
Come on friend, I double dare you. Are you coming?

STEP 1 – See yourself in a fresh way

When I realised it was time for me to switch sides, the first thing I had to do was to see myself in a fresh way. I had to stop focusing on my past. In fact I had to let go of my past to grab hold of my future. You are not a failure, failure is an event. We have all done some things that we are not proud of, but that's not who we are. The past is now history. As you know, my past did not determine my future and your past does not have to determine yours. There was a turning point for me, let your turning point be right now. Make this decision today: 'I have come this far and no further on the wrong side'. It is time to stop being negative and doing negative things. It is only a matter of time before your cup is full.
There is hope for you. So right now, say goodbye to your past and hello to your future.

I had to picture in my mind what I really wanted. I had to get alone to do this. I had to decide what I wanted to focus on. I got myself a picture board, put it in my room and put pictures and words on it that would help me to focus. You can do the same. Put on the picture board your dream car and your dream home. What is your dream job or business? Where are your dream holiday resorts and countries? Who are those you would one day like to meet? Who are those you want to make proud of you? Maybe it's your family; put them on your picture board also. This and much more you can put on your board and every day look at it and say, 'coming soon'. This will keep you excited and focused.

Before you start throwing tomatoes at me, if you have never tried it, you don't qualify to tell me that it does not work.

There is a high tendency that what you picture in your mind and speak with your mouth, you will reproduce. So I had to get a positive self-image of myself and my future. I know some of these statements may sound really off-key and unusual. This sort of stuff is generally not taught in school. Once again, it worked for me and it is still working for me. I don't see why it won't work for you. Besides, I can only give you what I have. In fact, these steps will work for young people and adults. I continue to use them myself. There are certain principles that are not respecters of people - if you use them, they work irrespective of colour, creed, age, race or sex.

To round off this step, I need you to recognise that you can do anything you put your heart and mind to. Whatever you focus on, you become. So if you focus on your past, you will stay there, if you focus on your future, you will arrive there. Get your perspective right or die trying.

STEP 2 – Hang out with the right crowd

I realised that if I was really going to switch sides, there would have to be some major changes with those I spent time with. There is power in association. Your associations are either positive or negative. You can either fly with eagles or hang around with ducks. My dad always used to say, "Tell me who you go with and I will tell you what you are and what your future holds". I used to think "whatever", but I have now found this to be very true. I have also heard it said, "If I meet your family, that explains your past and present, but if I meet your friends, that explains your future". It is hard to argue with that.

Young people find this hard to accept, but do you know how many young people are in jail for crimes they did not commit? They were at the wrong place at the wrong time with the wrong people.

So many young people have been killed because they were seen with a particular person that had enemies. Some of you that are innocent have been labelled as criminals, gang bangers and easy-lays because of the people you hang with and the company you keep.

This is serious, so please don't take it lightly. Choose your friends wisely. Anyone not adding to you is taking away from you. So my question to you is, "who are you hanging with?" The truth is you are going to mirror the people you choose to spend time with.

I took and sold drugs because of those I chose to hang out with, that's what they did. But the funny thing is that I ended up in prison, some of them did not.

Young people hear me out for a second, we generally think parents and teachers don't understand our reality, but the truth is they were once young and there is nothing new under the sun. There really is a lot of truth in what adults tell us. Please take it on board before you dismiss their words of wisdom. Yes, they sometimes give advice from a standpoint of fear, but they generally want the best for us. Parents do make mistakes. That's the world we live in, but remember, there is no manual on how to be a great parent. Experience really is the best teacher, so why make the same mistakes somebody else has already made. You don't need to make the mistakes I have made. Take it from me, it's not all that.

A few years ago, my phone used to ring more than forty times a day, now it does not ring more than ten times, and that's including business. In the past, a lot of my associations were negative, fruitless and unfulfilling. Now people need to qualify for my association and people need to qualify for yours. That's not arrogance, that's being wise about who you let into your inner circle. Not everyone should have access to you. I had to rid myself of every association that was negative. Your life and time is too precious. Not everyone that knows you should be called your friend. I choose to hang out with winners, champions, people that have goals and dreams and work towards them daily.

Funnily enough, I now choose not to associate with those that break the law. It took a lot of work and effort to gain people's trust again and there is no association worth me tarnishing my image and defaming my character. I choose to hang with people that are going somewhere, people that I can believe in and people that believe in me.

I have friends whose lives were cut short because of wrong association. A word is enough for the wise. With the right people in your circle, you can do great things. Check yourself, check your friends. Get your association right or die trying.

STEP 3 - Check your attitude

As I went through various trials, here is what I realised: nobody in life owed me anything. My biggest enemy was the person that looked back at me when I looked in the mirror. Wherever you are in your life right now is based on the thoughts and decisions you have made. Your actions are a product of your thoughts and your thoughts are a product of your association and all other forms of exposure such as friendships, family, TV, radio and Internet.

I had a choice as to what I allowed myself to become exposed to. It hit me that positive exposure would produce positive results and negative exposure would produce negative results. It's that simple really.

It all came down to my attitude. Your attitude is everything. Check yourself, check your attitude.

I had to ask those around me to be really honest with me. I needed them tell me what I was really like without the fear of me being offended. I was not asking for criticism, but I did need feedback. Your energy, actions and the way you carry yourself is all connected to your attitude. You are either going to attract the right people and the right opportunities to you or you are going to repel people and opportunities from you. For so long, I had attracted the wrong people and the wrong opportunities.

Everything you do in life, its success and failure has a lot to do with your attitude.
How you relate to people, family, friends, teachers, employers and anyone else all comes down to your attitude. Don't miss this, this is crucial.

So I had to get real honest with myself, maybe you should also. If you were somebody else, would you like to hang around with you? Would you have someone like you as a friend? It really is all about attitude. I hated being corrected or criticised. How well do you take correction? I always had to be right, do you? I was a really selfish person. Are you a giver or just a taker? I did not have much respect for those older than me, even though I had been brought up with those principles. Do you respect those older than you? I know that's not popular in this day and age, but we need to show a level of respect to those older than us.

I have a driver who works for me; he is old enough to be my dad. Yes he works for me, I pay his salary but I would never disrespect him. It is good to give honour to whom honour is due. Respect will get you real far in life. Yes, it is give and take but are you willing to give it first? It all comes down to attitude. When things did not go my way, I would sulk and have a pity party rather than shake off my frustration and get on with things. I used to murmur and complain at the slightest discomfort instead of taking things in my stride.
When you have a bad attitude, you will generally make bad decisions. Are you aware of your attitude? You need to be aware of your attitude everyday, in all you do and wherever you go. You never know when an opportunity is about to show up. Get your attitude right or die trying.

STEP 4 - Believe in yourself
There came a point when I started to realise that I did not have much faith in my own ability or who I was as a person. The day I attended the church in East London, one of the things that Pastor Matthew said that struck me was, "if it's going to be, it's up to me". I needed to start believing in myself. If you don't have any belief in you, then you better go and buy some. As we all know, you can't buy belief, but you do have to start believing in you. If you don't, why should anyone else? If you think you are a loser, why should I think differently? You must believe that you can and you have the ability to achieve all you set your heart and mind to do. You must believe that you can do well in your academics, in sports, in performing and in your work or business.

Whatever it is, you must believe in you and the ability on the inside of you. When you have the 'fear and failure are not options' mindset, you will make maximum impact and achieve what you have never achieved before.

No matter the mistakes you have made in the past, you have got to believe in you. As I said, your past does not have to determine your future. Having belief in yourself puts you in an advantageous position and builds your foundation for success.

For some reason, the older we get, the less people believe in us. It is nice and helpful when we have people that believe in us, but if there is no one to believe in you, you can't give up on yourself. If there is no one to encourage you, you must encourage yourself. If you have to look in the mirror and speak to yourself, then that's what it's going to take. I do that whenever I am feeling a bit low.

Sometimes people find themselves discouraging others without realising the impact of their words. The words of negative, pessimistic people can be like poison. If you can't encourage someone or give them constructive feedback, please shut your mouth. I have to say it that strongly because every day, talent is dying because of what people have said. The worst is when a parent or teacher discourages a young person. That is a capital offence as far as I'm concerned. Parents should not download their negative experiences and expectations onto their children. I have said it on numerous occasions, because that is what a lot of parents find themselves subconsciously doing. By this action, a child has already been placed in a mental and emotional prison. A parent's experience does not have to be a child's reality.

Other people that can discourage you are friends that don't want to think big for themselves. They would rather you stayed like them. That's another friend that needs to be expelled from your inner circle or side-stepped. You would have noticed that eagles don't fly with ducks and chickens. Don't let people clip your wings if you want to fly. It's okay to believe in your dreams.

Have you been dreaming lately?

If you can conceive an idea, believe it. I promise you, you can achieve it. There's something else I need you to know - IT'S POSSIBLE. You can be all you want to be. The truth is that there will be times when you will not be able to depend on anyone but yourself. So if you don't have belief in yourself that may become a problem. Believing in you is critical. Don't let anybody steal the belief that you have in yourself. When you have no belief in yourself, when things get hard, you will quit. Quitters never win and winners never quit. When you quit, you miss out on opportunities that may never come round again.

Let me give you an example. From an early age, I was a very good football player. Scouts were hunting me down from the age of 11. They were coming to my school and to my home. My Dad never welcomed scouts and he never welcomed the idea of me becoming a footballer. My Dad once got really angry with a scout and was on the verge of attacking him, when my Mum had to stand between them. Football was not encouraged in our household. It was all about education. We were made to study every day. My Dad was of the view that when you are eating breakfast, lunch or dinner that was more than enough recreation.

I was always told that if I broke my leg playing football or destroyed my knee, then that would be the end of my life. So I was never totally committed to football, but I was not committed to my studies either because all I could think about was football. This obviously had an impact on me subconsciously. So nothing ever had my full attention. This meant that I played football with a 'what if?' attitude. I also studied with the same attitude. This led to me doubting my ability in both areas. It was only a matter of time before I was no longer the footballer I used to be, and of course my grades did not get any better either.

Against all odds you must believe in you and never doubt your own ability. Even if everyone says you can't, if you say you can, then friend, you truly can.

STEP 5 – Feed your mind

Even though I had now decided to switch sides, I had a major inferiority complex. I did not feel comfortable going for job interviews or answering questions in public. My vocabulary was limited which limited me mentally and otherwise. My Dad had always encouraged me to read books for fun, but it was not for me. It did not fit in with my other ventures and lifestyle. Being bright was not cool. But I was in a new season and things had to really change, especially my mind.

One day I was standing at a bus stop and there was an elderly man sitting there waiting for his bus. As our eye's made contact he smiled at me. I did not smile back. After a few minutes had passed, the elderly man turned to me and said, "Young man, readers are leaders, the more you learn, the more you earn. The less you learn, the less you earn". As those words came out of his mouth, it was like a switch had been turned on. Wow! Why had nobody ever said it like this before? I now smiled back at the elderly man and told him thank you. He said, "I can see that you are a rough diamond, those that don't read depend on those that do". A few weeks after that Pastor Matthew repeated words along those same lines. That is when I made a decision to keep educating myself for the rest of my life. Lifelong learning will keep you growing.

A few years ago, I would never have been able to write a book. A few years ago, I probably felt the same way about reading as some of you do. I'm sure you have heard that knowledge is power. The more you read, the more your mind is developed. If you already read, please don't stop. If you don't read, please get started. Initially, I did not enjoy reading. The more I kept with it, the easier it became for me. Here I am now, writing my second book. Remember I had dyslexia and was not considered to be very bright in school. I'm sure many of you were like me. I would start a book and never get past chapter two. If I knew what I know now, I would have got into reading a lot earlier.

Readers can have super confidence. Readers are better thinkers and generally have more options. When you read, it gives you insight into the lives of others. When you read biographies, motivational and self-help books like this one, you are standing on the shoulders of those that have gone before you. In a few hours, you are getting the experience that took the author twenty or thirty years to get. When you read, you can learn from other people's mistakes and avoid some of their failures. When you read a book by a successful person that you admire, you will see the road map to get to where they are with less hassle, drama and traffic. I also enjoy reading the Bible because it gives so much guidance and direction to young people. Let me set the record straight here. Reading is really important. Take advantage of reading today. Reading will give you the belief that you can pursue the picture in your mind.

Now I hear you saying, 'There's so many books out there, how do I know what to read?' Some people like to sit on the fence here, but I can't and won't do that. We are talking about staying out of trouble. I do not think you should read whatever you like. Whether we like it or not, not everything is good for us. Let's be honest, we all know that not all books are good for us. Three things will determine where you will be this time next year:

What you watch and who you watch;
What you listen to and who you listen to;
What you read.

There are books that will lead you down the wrong road and, if you have read this far, then I trust you have enough discernment, intelligence and wisdom to make the right decision. Remember: cause and effect, action and reaction. What you read will affect your thinking, which will determine your actions and in turn cause a reaction. It's your call, but only you will pay the price and only you will reap what you sow, whether positively or negatively.

The kinds of books that I recommend are life and self-improvement books - books that empower you and aid personal development. Novels can also be helpful in improving your vocabulary. Biographies are usually easy to read and give a lot of insight into the realities of life. People's stories are easy to relate to. I always want to know how certain people made it in life against all odds. The first section of this book is about me, but it's also about you. You don't have to go through what I have been through. You can make fewer mistakes and have fewer failures. It's always interesting finding out what people had to go through to get where they are. Reading will empower you and enforce the feeling that you can move from mediocrity to winning in life.

The more information we get in our minds about our dreams, goals, career plans and targets, the quicker we can get from where we are to where we really want to be. Remember, 'readers are leaders' and 'the more you learn, the more you earn'. Once you finish this book, you need to start thinking about the next book you are going to read. Twenty to thirty minutes of reading a day will transform how you think and act in twenty-one days. But don't forget, get the right books.

Over the last five years, I have read at least five hundred books and they all have impacted how I think, act and live. But if there is one book that stands out for me, it is definitely the Bible. It is totally amazing. It has given me insight, clarity and understanding into the issues and battles of life. It does not stop there, it also gives you numerous keys for every aspect of your life that will unlock your potential and empower you to move past your pain and step into the next level of living. Unlike all the other books, the Bible is a book that you can pick up every day and it will teach you mind blowing new things on a daily basis.

I know there is a view amongst young people and adults that the Bible is not relevant to today's society. You could not be further from the truth. There are so many versions and translations that speak everyday English which is so easy to understand. The Message Translation, for example, reads like a novel.

Ted Turner, founder and owner of the CNN news channel is a known atheist, but he has read the Bible from the beginning to the end, twice. Whatever your faith, irrespective of what you believe in or don't believe in, the Bible is a book that can touch parts of your life that, up until now, have appeared untouchable and unchangeable. If there's one book that has my total seal of approval, then it's the B.I.B.L.E (Basic instructions before leaving earth) go get your copy today.
Start reading today and check yourself in twelve months. You will definitely notice how far you have come and what you have become.
Now I want you to remember this: a person that does not read has no advantage over a person that cannot read. So, I ask you, what's your excuse?

STEP 6 – Follow your dreams
Any dream you do not fulfil may eventually become a nightmare. As I said earlier, I had the potential and was on my way to becoming a pre-

miership footballer, but I did not make it. I did not make it not because I wasn't good enough, but because I did not try hard enough. I liked the dreams of becoming a premiership footballer but I cannot say that I was willing to pay the price. Every dream has a cost and you must be willing to pay the price. Remember, there are two types of pain in life - the pain of discipline and the pain of regret. Regret hurts much more. That's when you start singing, 'I should have, would have, could have'. And the bottom line is nobody really cares.

You will only be remembered in life for what you were able to do and not what you planned to do. You have to make a conscious decision to follow, focus and stick with your dreams. You must do so today. I will give you this for free: no one said it's going to be easy. If it was easy, everybody would be doing what you want to do. There are some things and some places you must go through on the journey towards living your dream. In anything of note, there are phases. A butterfly goes through phases. A man was first a baby, then a toddler, then an infant, and so on, before he became a man. Any champion of worth was first a challenger. Any king was first a prince. I'm sure you get the message, so here's what I'm saying, in regards to fulfilling your dream, know that you will go from the dream phase, to the struggle phase to the victory phase. On my journey to becoming a premiership footballer, I never made it out of the struggle phase.

You must see your dream through to the end. Quitting cannot and should never be the option. Quitters never win and winners never quit. If you don't believe in yourself and your dream why should anybody else? If it's going to happen, then it's up to you. You must do all that is within your power to achieve your dream. You must make sure you don't let anyone or anything stop you. You need to have tunnel vision. The storm may rage, the sea might roar, but you must decide that your dream will not be killed or stolen.

People may talk, that's up to them. It's always better to be in the action than to be watching from the sidelines. Let me give you an example. For me, watching golf or cricket is extremely boring, but playing it is something completely different. Be a player and not a couch critic. Get in the game of life and follow your dream.

At times it may look like the dream is over, but you must remember that if you conceive an idea and believe the idea, then you can achieve it. Yes you can! You can do anything if you try. Trials will come and go, but the trials will just make you stronger and give you a sure foundation.

Do not fear, stand tall but keep moving forward. Anyone you celebrate and admire today started with a dream. They went through the process of struggling until they become victorious. For you to make it and fulfil your dream, you will have to go through the same phases. But I promise you it's worth it. You will hit walls and be met with resistance; people may ridicule you, laugh at you and tell you that you're a joker. You will be told, it's not possible and it's never been done before. If I could look you in the eyes right now, I would say one thing… follow your dreams because they are achievable. If anyone can, you can. If you are willing to stay on course, stay persistent and stay focused, the dream is yours. You may get knocked down, but refuse to get knocked out. Victory awaits you, a standing ovation awaits you, fulfilment awaits you and success is calling you. On your marks, get set, GO…

STEP 7 – Don't let obstacles hold you back

Following right on from the last step - tough times don't last but tough people do. A wise man once said, "hard times are never here to stay… they are only here to pass". Whatever problems you face, this too shall come to pass. The truth is every problem has an expiry date. That includes yours as well. Hard times, dry seasons and obstacles are not necessarily bad things because they strengthen you. We all go through, have gone through and will go through obstacles. You can't afford to give up or throw in the towel when conditions are not favourable. It is part of the process on the way to where you are going. I have been through so many tough times but I'm still standing.

I anticipate more obstacles on the way and I will overcome them also.

No obstacle is big enough to stop me and no obstacle is big enough to stop you. Yes, at times it may not feel that way but as long as you have a never-say-never attitude, you will be just fine. Having dyslexia was an obstacle, having low self-esteem was a major obstacle. At times being black in the estate we lived in was an obstacle. Having a criminal record was an obstacle. Having a bad temper was an obstacle. Hanging with the wrong crowd and being influenced by peer pressure was an obstacle. I had many childhood experiences that were obstacles but I had a choice, I could let the obstacles keep me down or I could choose to overcome the obstacles.

You see, we all have obstacles, it's what we choose to do with them that matters. We can give them permanent residence in our lives or we can choose to evict them. We need to become solution oriented and not problem focused. I did and you can do the same.

Sometimes we wonder, 'Why is all this happening to me?' There are times we go through one problem after another and there are times when we have multiple issues all at the same time. We believe, 'this is the one that's going to kill me, I'm never going to get out of this, I'm finished and it's all over now'. The simple fact of life is they are just obstacles. You can go round an obstacle, you can go over an obstacle, you can knock it down and sometimes you can even go under it. Each problem has a solution and the problem is never final unless you say so. The more you talk about a problem, the more power you give it. There are some obstacles that don't even deserve your attention. Obstacles are just one of the signposts we see along the way, on our journey to fulfilling our dreams and destiny.

Remember, hard times, dry seasons and obstacles are friends in disguise. They will propel you to your next level. I have survived them and you will also.

Don't forget, you only become a champion by going through certain fights and battles. No pain, no gain. No story, no glory.
Andrew Nwachukwu - I will never forget you:

I remember in 2003 I was sitting down having a discussion with my Dad when the phone rang. It was my friend Yvonne. She told me to sit down that she had some serious news to share with me. I did not take her seriously at first because Yvonne always had news to tell me. She always seemed to be the one that knew what was going on before anyone else. So I said, "What is it this time?" and she said, "Sit down please". I could hear her crying and that's when I knew that this was not going to be the usual chit-chat.

Her next words made me hit the floor instantly and I shouted, "NO! NO! NO!" Yvonne told me that she was at Saint Thomas' hospital in London and my cousin Andrew had lost his battle with Sickle Cell. My Dad understood why I was shouting and he collapsed into his chair. It was a real sad day. After I was able to get myself together, I picked myself up from the floor and my brother Leo and I drove to the hospital. When we arrived, there were so many young people on the hospital corridors crying and consoling each other. As we began hugging everyone and anyone, tears started streaming down my face again. I could not control myself.

I went in to see Andrew's body and he lay there smiling and at peace. For the next two weeks, hundreds of young people would gather every night at Andrew's mum's house to bond, share, eat, laugh and cry.

I was asked to be the Master of Ceremony at the wake/funeral so I went about planning how to make it a unique and special day. I tried to write a speech. Andrew was all about peace, love and unity and that is how he spent his last days, reaching out and encouraging us all to live in harmony and love. He celebrated friendship and brotherhood and detested hate, jealousy, anger and violence.

On the night of the wake, I decided to give the speech I had written with hundreds of friends, family, mourners and well wishers locked in a chain all holding hands.

For those few moments we were all one. Enmity and hate was put on hold as we all merged and became a unit where nothing else mattered.

I gave my first prepared speech and ended with all the young people coming together singing songs and clapping in unison. What a moment, what an experience.

My speaking career began at Andrew's wake. That night, hundreds of people told me that was what I was supposed to be doing. I guess in those few moments the crowd were inspired and empowered. That night I decided to investigate the world of public speaking. Did Andrew have to die for me to realise my potential? That is a question I ask myself every time I have a microphone in my hand or I am standing on a platform. I know if he was here, he would say "cous, go for it and deliver with excellence, go out there and love those people with your words, make a difference now and make maximum impact". I have no doubt God gives him sneak previews of what is going on down here and I hope he is proud and smiling like only he could.

Andrew, we still miss you very much and you are constantly on our minds. You may not be with us, but you still live on. If it was down to us, you would still be here with us, but you have gone to a better place where there is no hate, anger or violence. Till we meet again, rest in peace. We love you.

STEP 8 – Find mentors and role models

As my life started to turn around, certain things still did not make sense. I had so many questions that still needed answering and I knew that on my own, there was only so far I could go. By this point I had chosen various fields I wanted to be successful in. So I knew that I needed to surround myself with successful people who knew what I did not know, people who were already authorities in the areas that were important to me.

You need mentors and positive role models. Not anyone and everyone can be your mentor. Who you allow mentor you is a decision that you cannot take lightly. It is ever so important to have mentors and positive role models in your life. Find someone doing what you want to do, how you want to do it, at the level you want to do it and study their success because success leaves clues.

There are a few things you should consider when choosing mentors and role models. Is the person's attitude worth catching? Does the person believe in you? Does the person have integrity? Is the person of good character? Is the person willing to develop you? Does the person have relevant experience? Is the person still growing themselves?

A mentor or role model should have certain qualities. Your mentor should be a good listener. Your mentor should be non-judgmental. Your mentor should have empathy and be supportive. Your mentor should be available and accessible. A good mentor has the ability to ask the right questions. A quality mentor is able to build rapport.

Some of us know what we want to do and where we want to go, but we are not sure how to get there. That's what a mentor will do for you. There is someone who has already walked in the shoes you are trying to walk in. Know that your mentor had to go through many things to get where he or she is today. Now whatever field you want to go into, there is a mentor out there for you.

Do you want to be a singer, actor or sportsman? Then find people that have been or are successful in that area or field. If you want to be a lawyer, doctor, accountant or engineer, there are many successful ones out there that are willing to share their experiences, know-how and time with you.

When I knew that I wanted to become an Inspirational and Empowerment Speaker, I tracked down a man by the name of Richie Dayo Johnson and from there joined a Toastmasters' club. It was as simple as that. Since then, I have been privileged to be inspired and impacted by many other speakers. I try to listen to someone every day. I don't only get mentored by people I meet personally, but I also get mentored by people whose tapes and CDs I listen to. I get mentored by the people whose DVDs I watch and of course, I get mentored by the people whose books I read. Whose books are you reading? Who and what are you watching and who are you listening to?

These are major questions. Now I have mentors for most parts of my life. I have speaking mentors, business mentors, relationship mentors, spiritual mentors, money mentors, and personal mentors. All of these mentors help keep my life balanced. I need them to keep doing what I'm doing. You may have to track your mentors down as I did. Initially they may not show interest in you but be persistent. Don't take any form of rejection personal. That's life. Just don't back down if that is the right mentor for you.

When you have the opportunity to finally get your mentors attention, just keep it simple. Greet them, tell them your name and say something along the lines of 'you're doing what I want to do, you have touched lives. You have touched my life, you have changed my life, please can you help me. You don't have to do anything for me, I just need some tips and advice every now and then. Anything you are willing to share with me will be much appreciated.'

Pastor Matthew is my mentor that speaks to me from the pulpit most Sundays. Les Brown, Brian Tracy, Zig Ziglar and Bob Proctor are mentors that speak to me through their books and podcasts. Atiti Sosimi of Distinctly Different is a mentor that I speak to on the phone every once in a while. Justin Smith of Youth media is a mentor that I have a coffee with every three months, usually early in the morning at a Coffee Republic or a Starbucks. I cannot mention all the people that have had a hand in the man I have become today. There is an African proverb that says 'it takes a village to raise a child'. Many hands have linked together to build and restructure my life. To every mentor and helper, I salute you and I will forever remain grateful. Thank you.

Who around you is doing what you want to do? Make contact today. You have to start building relationships with those people so that you can get the coaching and training you need to fulfill your dream. Now is not the time to be fearful. Be bold and courageous and make it happen. You never know, you might share the stage with them one day.

STEP 9 – Know who you are

Inside you is a winner. Inside you there is a champion and that is who you really are. You must always listen to the victor in you and put the victim to death. Yes you have been through certain experiences, but that does not have to determine what you do, who you are and what you become. Sometimes negative voices speak too loud. We all have doubts and fears, but we must override those feelings. Let me put it this way, you must learn to doubt your doubts. Whatever it is, feel the fear and do it anyway.

We tend to focus on the negative voice quite a lot, but the negative voice has nothing to offer you. The negative voice says, what if? Are you sure? Maybe not now, what about if it does not work? What about if I fail? The negative voice will keep you stagnant; the negative voice will keep you from stepping out of the comfort zone. The negative voice can come from our family and friends: you can't do it, you're not old enough, you don't have enough experience, you're black, you're white, you're too fat, you're a lady etc.

Usually, that voice can be so overwhelming that we give up even before we get started. But there is another voice that says, I can do this, I'm more than able, if anyone can, I can, nothing is going to stop me, it's my time, I'm going for it, I can make this happen, if it's been done before, I can do it too, if it has not been done before I can also do it.

I want you to know that's the voice you need to listen to, that's the voice that loves you, that's the voice that wants to see you at the top. The negative voice is comfortable with the way things are.

We usually pick the easy way out, but if you have read this far, then you must be hungry, you must want more than you have right now. Now I encourage you, make it happen.

After coming out of prison, people told me that there was no hope for me. I was told that I would be broke for the rest of my life unless I went back to crime and drug dealing. And truly, that was the easier option; I already knew how to beat the system. You did not need any qualifications to sell drugs. But I was tired of looking behind my back everywhere I went. I was tired of pretending to be angry even when I was not. I was tired of faking it. I was tired of sleepless nights. I was tired of cheating and hurting people.

I decided I was going to make an honest living even if it was uncomfortable. I went back to walking and catching the bus and the train instead of driving in cars that were dodgy and doctored. I went back to buying clothes in markets instead of designer labels with fake credit cards. I decided to go back to school. I decided to get a job and then another job. And then I started a cleaning business and then a security company and then a bar tending business. Now I am a Toastmaster of ceremonies, speaker, trainer, learning mentor and author.

Now remember, this is a man whose CV read, drug dealer, gang member, fraudster, criminal and so on.

We all have different stories, but in some ways they are all similar. Some of us had bad starts in life, but we can trade that for a better future. And if you have had a good start in life, don't take it for granted.

If I am living a life that some may feel that I do not deserve, considering my track record, what about you? You can live your dream if you listen to the winner in you. You can do anything you want to do if you set your mind to it. You must be willing to take a chance on yourself. People always tell us to take care and to be cautious, I say take charge, you are a winner and you better believe that. Hear me out, I believe in you, but the question is do you believe in yourself. Once again, trade where you are for where you really want to be. Trade your liabilities for assets. Trade doubt for hope. Trade laziness for diligence. Trade a bad character for a good attitude. Finally, trade the mind set of a loser for the vision and passion of a champion and world beater.

BONUS STEPS

STEP 10 – Dress for Success

Of course, as a young person I used to be really conscious of my image but I still had poor self-esteem. I used to love wearing baggy jeans, boots or trainers with a hooded top and a big jacket. Wearing bulky clothes was useful for many reasons. Even dressing a particular way helped you to command more respect on the street. But in all honesty, it was not respect. We dressed to intimidate. Did it work? I would say yes, because there were times when people would scan you with their eyes and think twice about stepping to a confrontation.

The hood for example is part fashion statement, part camouflage against C C T V, the police and potential enemies. It is also a deterrent to others to think twice. If I did not have a hood on, then a face cap would be my choice of the day.
I had my reasons for wearing such attire, but not everyone that wears this kind of clothing is a gang member or a thug up to no good. A lot of young people feel wrongly judged just because of their attire and how they dress. Right now wearing a hood or other related clothing signifies being a rough tough kid, but what you wear does not necessarily signify who you are.

I am not sure if it is right to judge people based on how they dress, but the bottom line is we are judged within fifteen seconds of standing before people. People make a decision about you before they hear what you have to say. How you dress does project an image. Whether we like it or not, how you dress is always taken into consideration. Your dress code can give you a competitive edge when looking for work or it can be the reason for your elimination.

I have come to understand, through personal experience, that dressing appropriately is majorly important. There is an old adage that says you never get a second chance to make a first impression. You do not have to spend a fortune to look good.

Here are a few tips that will help you to dress for success:

Have a spotless, polished, and conservative look.
Hair should be professional and well-groomed.

All applicants need professional and conservative shoes.
Clean teeth and fresh breath are critical.
There should be no strong smelling perfumes/colognes, after shave, or scented lotions.
Fingernails and toenails should be clean, trimmed, and women should have a conservative-coloured nail polish.
Both men and women should have a minimal amount of jewellery on. A classy and professional look is the goal.
Obviously, ensure that body odour is not an issue. If you live in a hot environment you can always bring a small, travel-sized deodorant with you.
There should be no gum, candy, items to chew, or tongue piercing during the interview.
There should be, at most, one pair of earrings on and no other visible piercing. If men want to wear earrings they should be small and professional.
Try to cover tattoos. Most of our society has changed their views on tattoos, but there are some who do not want tattoos presented at work.
Buying a professional wardrobe does not have to be expensive. Most of the department stores that have expensive clothing have great sale racks. There are discount department stores that offer name-brand, professional clothes with inexpensive prices. You can also visit department store websites. They often offer a large amount of clearance clothing with low shipping charges. Affordable clothing is available and you can inexpensively dress for success.

Now I hear somebody saying, I want to dress how I like. You have the right to do that, but you then limit your ability to get the ultimate jobs and positions that are desired. That's just the way it is. It basically comes down to looking and feeling confident, determined and professional.

Now as a speaker and trainer, I am very conscious of what I wear at all times. It can sometimes be the deciding factor of whether I am given a contract or speaking slot, I am sure. I agree that it is the man that wears the clothes and not vice versa, but I can confidently say that your clothes do speak on your behalf. I have also noticed that certain clothes affect how I stand and how I walk. So these days, it would be hard for you to find me in boots, baggy jeans and a hood. Dressing right pays.

We all have particular styles and fashions that we favour, but the bottom line is to dress appropriately and dress for where you are going and not for where you are. Your appearance and clothes simply advertise you before you open your mouth.

STEP 11 – Learn to communicate effectively

Miscommunication has become the norm of the day. As a gang member and drug dealer, I had mastered the art of street lingo and slang. Speaking that way served me well on the streets and in clubs but this sort of language was not going to help me to get out of trouble and stay out of trouble. As I went about living a negative life and hanging around negative company, I pretended to be confident. I faked self-esteem, self belief and self knowledge.

My language and vocabulary was poor, my grammar embarrassed me and my communication skills were not advertising me well.
Even when I knew it was time for a change, I did not have much to work with. I would go for jobs and be turned down on a regular basis. This would annoy me and I was sometimes quick to play the race card. On reflection, it was not race but how I came across, how I carried myself and how I communicated.

As I said earlier, once I decided to improve on my communication skills, I tracked down Richie Dayo Johnson and he took me to Toastmasters International. A not-for-profit organisation that now has nearly 235,000 members all over the world offering a proven and enjoyable way to practice and hone communication and leadership skills.
As a speaker and trainer, the ability to communicate is vital to my success. It is also how I earn a living, so I will always be a champion for effective speaking and communication. Well delivered words can influence, motivate and inspire.

I love speaking in public and class myself as fortunate to be able to do for a living what I would be willing to do for free. I do not take it lightly when people sit before me and lend me their ears.

I encourage you to improve on your communication skills. Whenever you are speaking, your content, delivery and structure determines whether you get the desired result. Sometimes we get into confrontations and misunderstandings because communication has been poor. Communication is not just speaking, but also listening and body language. At least seventy-five percent of communication is non-verbal.

If we all became better listeners and better speakers, there would be less problems in our homes, communities, schools, at work and there would be less wars both locally and internationally.
Clubs and Organisations like Toastmasters are springing up everywhere. As I said, a better future begins with a better you. Organisations like this will help you to communicate more effectively, become a better listener, improve your presentation skills, increase your leadership potential, increase your self confidence and you will build your ability to motivate and persuade.

Young people who speak and communicate well really have a head start and a heads up. Quality communication makes the difference when it comes to anger management and conflict resolution.

The usual case with communication skills is that most people assume that they make themselves clear and are easy to understand so if there's a problem, it's with the other person, not us. We are always quick to blame the other person. How often do we hear the words, 'but I thought you meant' or 'no you have completely misunderstood me'. We need to make ourselves clear and get ourselves understood and at the same time, we need to be clear about what others are saying and understand them also.

Poor communication has led to divorce, deaths, wars and breakdowns in various types of relationships. A few tips that make the difference are: learning to pause, make eye contact, be yourself, speak up and speak out, let your words be structured, pace yourself and keep it simple. Communication skills are not something that should be left to chance.

Well done for walking through the steps to getting out and staying out of trouble. Of course, there are more than these eleven steps to succeed in your life and become all you want to be. But it will move you forward along the way. I invite you to revisit this book once in a while and try and start to implement the steps immediately. It will not happen overnight. It is a gradual process. Slow and steady wins the race. You may fall at times, but get back up again. At times it may feel like you are not making progress, but stay on course and keep focused. Armed with all this information, you must take responsibility for your decisions and actions. I am speaking to you from personal experience. I try my best to follow these nine steps and I will for the rest of my life. I am still growing and with every day that passes, I become a better person. You don't have to prove anything to anyone but yourself. Let your life speak for you.

You may have heard this before: on your gravestone when you die, there will be two dates, the year you were born and the year you died. There is a hyphen or a dash in between the two dates. The hyphen is really asking one question, 'What did you do with your life?' Let your life count for something. Let your name mean something. How will you like to be remembered when you are no longer here? As I have said before, when you die, will it even matter that you lived? Make the right decisions now, so that tomorrow will take care of itself. Get out and stay out of trouble. Let us now remind ourselves of the steps that we have learnt in this book.

STEP 1- Your past does not determine your future, so see yourself in a positive image and realise that today is a good day to start a new beginning and live a new life for the rest of your life.

STEP 2- There is power in association. If your friendships are not right, then you need to trade them for new ones. If you hang around dogs, then you will get fleas. Remember, eagles stick with eagles and not ducks.

STEP 3- You better check your attitude right now, if your attitude is wrong, then everything else is guaranteed to be wrong. Things will get better when you get better; a better future begins with a better you.

STEP 4- If you don't believe in yourself, don't expect anyone else to. Know that you were born to win. You just have to believe that you can do anything you set your mind to achieve.

STEP 5- Readers are leaders. The more you learn, the more you earn, the less you learn, the less you earn. Any person of note has kept on learning. If you want to start leading then you better start reading.

STEP 6- Dream big. Follow and chase down your dreams. It will happen if you stay on course. It will happen if you don't give up. It may take a while, but it's coming if you hang in there and keep pressing and pushing towards the finish line.

STEP 7- When tough times show up, make sure you do also. When the going gets tough, it's the time for you to get going. Tough times don't last, but tough people do. You are tough, brave and courageous. You are a victor and not a victim. Don't forget, every problem has an expiry date.

STEP 8- Your mentor is not your friend but the coach who wants to see you win in life. Your friends love you the way you are. Your mentor loves you too much to let you stay the same. You must choose your mentor wisely. You must also choose a mentor for the right reasons or else you will not get out and stay out of trouble.
STEP 9- Remember, you have value. You're a champion in the making. You're a mentor in training. You are success waiting to happen. You are not fearful. You are a barrier breaker, headliner and a line-crosser. There is a winner in you and the world is a waiting for you to express yourself.

STEP 10- Dressing appropriately is crucial. People will always focus on your appearance and the image you project and make judgement very quickly. Dressing right will give you a competitive edge especially when it comes to making initial impressions.

STEP 11- Being able to communicate effectively and efficiently is a visa to standing out and succeeding in your chosen field. Communicating well will help you get the things you want. Words carry power when used well. Words can cause problems if not delivered effectively.

You never know, we may one day cross paths. How do I know this? Because we are both on our way to the top, so I guess we might share an elevator.

You are my fellow survivor. I salute you and congratulate you on coming this far. Now let's cross the finish line.

Here's wishing you all the best, in all you do.

God Bless.

Kind Regards,

Charles Emeka

Pen Time

Part 2

1. Make a list of positive people in your life and list role models and mentors that can be of assistance to you

....
....
....
....
....
....
....
....
....
....
....
....
....
....
....
....
....
....
....
....
....
....
....
....
....
....
....
....
....
....

2. List your goals and aspirations for your life.

3. What steps and actions are you going to take to maximise and fulfill your potential.

4. Make a list of the things you have achieved in your life to date.

5. List five things that you can read to yourself daily that will empower, motivate, inspire and encourage you to keep focused and positive.

Charles Emeka has built his life and career on the wise words of great men and women. As a wise man once said, 'the pen is mightier than the sword'.

Below are quotes and statements that have been drawn from continuous study, research and life long learning. Some of the quotes will blow your mind and kick you into gear. Have fun.

Quotes for winners and those that want to stay on top:

"Change will not come if we wait for some other person or some other time. We are the ones we've been waiting for. We are the change that we seek".
Barack Obama

"One of the greatest tragedies in life is watching potential die
Dr Myles Munroe

"If you don't know who you are, other people will decide for you".
Matthew Ashimolowo

"There is a little difference in people, but that little difference makes a big difference. That little difference is attitude. The big difference is whether it is positive or negative".
W.Clement Stone

"People who soar, are those who refuse to sit back and wish things would change".
Charles R Swindoll

"Failure is an event, not a person. Yesterday ended last night".
Zig Ziglar

"Though no one can go back and make a brand new start, anyone can start from now and make a brand new ending".
Author Unknown

"A successful man is one who can build a firm foundation with the bricks that others throw at him".
David Brinkley

"When you blame others, you give up your power to change".
Dr Robert Anthony

"Any time you sincerely want to make a change, the first thing you must do is to raise your standards. When people ask me what really changed my life, I tell them that absolutely the most important thing was changing what I demanded of myself. I wrote down all the things I would no longer accept in my life, all the things I would no longer tolerate, and all the things that I aspired to becoming".
Anthony Robbins

"There are two primary choices in life, to accept conditions as they exist, or accept the responsibility for changing them".
Dennis Waitley

"Success is achieved by developing our strengths, not by eliminating our weaknesses".
Marilyn Vos Savant

A year from now you may wish you had started today.
Karen Lamb

"Anger makes you smaller, while forgiveness forces you to grow beyond what you were".
Cherie Carter- Scott

"And if the idea of having to change ourselves makes us uncomfortable, we can remain as we are. We can choose rest over labour, entertainment over education, delusion over truth, and doubt over confidence. The choices are ours to make. But while we curse the effect, we continue to nourish the cause".
Vic Johnson

"The road of average is paved by good intentions; the road of greatness is paved with action".
Author Unknown

"Principles without character is like a ship without water"
Robb Thompson

"Success is going from failure to failure without loss of enthusiasm".
Winston Churchill

"We all have ability; the difference is how we use it".
Stevie Wonder

"Holding anger is like grasping a hot coal with the intent of throwing it at someone else; you are the one who gets burned".
Author unknown

"Over sleeping will never make dreams come true"
Teen Esteem

"As we express our gratitude, we must never forget that the highest appreciation is not to utter words, but to live by them".
John F Kennedy

"You change your life by changing your choices".
Robb Thompson

"Ability is what you are capable of doing, motivation determines what you do, attitude determines how well you do it".
Lou Holtz

"To know where a person is coming from, look at their family. To know where a person is going to, look at their friends".
Unknown

"A pessimist sees the difficulty in every opportunity; an optimist sees the opportunity in every difficulty".
Winston Churchill

"Anyone who stops learning is old, whether at 20 or 80. Anyone who keeps learning stays young. The greatest thing in life is to keep your mind young".
Henry Ford

"You don't get paid for the hour; you get paid for the value you bring to the hour".
Jim Rohn

"It's not what has been done to you that seals the fate of your life but how you respond to injustice that determines your destiny".
Robb Thompson

The issues and battles of life are won and lost in the mind. In all you do, be the best and never forget that you were born to win.
Charles Emeka

"You take on the responsibility for making your dream a reality".
Les Brown

"Success does not come to you, you go to it".
Marva Collins

"Keep on going, and the chances are that you will stumble on something, perhaps when you are least expecting it. I never heard of anyone ever stumbling on something sitting down".
Charles F Kettering

Life takes on meaning when you become motivated, set goals and charge after them in an unstoppable manner.
Les brown

"If you are going through hell, keep going".
Winston Churchill

"Strength does not come from winning. Your struggles develop your strengths. When you go through hardships and decide not to surrender, that is strength".
Arnold Schwarzenegger

"We can throw stones, complain about them, stumble on them, climb over them, or build with them".
William Arthur ward

"He who gains a victory over other men is strong; but he who gains a victory over himself is all powerful".
Lao Tzu

"If you want to be remembered after your dead, write something worth reading or do something worth writing about".
Benjamin Franklin

"A man who ignores the truth is on a pathway to destruction".
Robb Thompson

"People can be divided into three groups, those who make things happen, those who watch things happen and those who wonder what happened".
John Newburn

Charles Emeka is a speaker, Toastmaster trainer and learning mentor that now spends his time speaking and training in conferences, schools, pupil referral units, prisons and in youth ministries.

If you would like Charles to come and facilitate/train or speak at your event or to a group of young people, please make contact via Charles Emeka International or Become Speakers and Mentors.

www.charlesemeka.com
www.become-sm.co.uk

Popular Presentations/Speeches

So you're about to finish school, now what you going to do? (Students)

The systems were wrong about me, are they wrong about you? (For All)

Destiny can't stop here (For All)

Things will go better, if I get better (For All)

How can you fly when you have already clipped your own wings (For All)

From victim to VICTOR (For All)

Raising Positive Children in a negative society (Teachers & Parents)

If it's going to be, it's up to me (students)

Attitude is everything (For All)

Life after school (Students)

Stay on the course-FOCUS (Students)

Being a bright light in a dark world (For All)

You were born to win (Students)

Be the best teacher here (Teachers)

Educators-Shapers of the dream (Teachers)

Your brain is your best weapon (Students)

When the drum beat changes, dance a different dance (For All)

Yes YOU can (Students)

Opportunity is staring you in the face (Students)

The only limitations are the ones you place on yourself (Students)

Education is First (Students)

Achieving Academic excellence (Students)

What's your excuse (For All)

Team Work/Unity/Agreement (For All)

PEAK: Passion, Excellence, Attitude, Knowledge (For All)

Internal Prisons (For All)

Dear Teacher, you were wrong about me (Students)

Purpose and identity (For all)

Ten Day Challenge (For all)

Our Parents got divorced, now what? (Students)

Programs

Public Speaking:
Public speaking is an art that is beneficial to every individual. This workshop will increase the confidence of pupils making them more comfortable with their fellow colleagues. It will also help individuals fine-tune their verbal communication skills.

Peer Pressure:
Peer Pressure is something young people deal with on a daily basis. At times peers can influence each other in negative ways. The idea that 'everyone's doing it' can lead to some kids making poor choices. The aim of this workshop is to help individuals develop a value system, a good sense of self and self worth.

Bullying:
ChildLine received over 31,000 bullying related calls last year from children and young people. Bullying can cause significant damage to the lives of young people. This workshop addresses why bullying takes place and teaches individuals how to detect early signs of it.

Conflict Management/Anger/Resolution:
The first step towards managing anger is to obtain an understanding of its root. A large number of youth battle with anger. We must help young people make sense of what is happening to them, and work with them to find alternative and appropriate ways to deal with their emotions. This workshop aims to equip individuals with effective skills for resolving conflicts and managing emotions.

Gangs, Violence, Gun Crime and weapons:
Youth gangs and violence has increased rapidly within our current communities. The government has great concern about the number of young people carrying both authentic and imitated weapons. This workshop reveals the ills and trappings of gangs, and will be beneficial for those who battle with anti-social behaviour.

Drugs/Alcohol and its effects:
Drugs and alcohol misuse is an ongoing problem. Many drugs taken for recreational reasons are illegal and can have serious negative consequences. Also alcohol abuse continues to be one of the most significant risk behaviours engaged in by teens. This workshop is designed to give pupils a real understanding of the negative effects of drugs and alcohol abuse.

Truancy:
Over 50,000 pupils miss at least a day of school without permission. Children who are not in school are vulnerable and more susceptible to crime, anti-social behaviour and future unemployment. The aim of this workshop is to inform individuals of the importance of education.

Self-esteem & Confidence:
Many young people suffer from low self-esteem and lack of confidence. Low self-esteem can stem from being harshly criticized, ignored, yelled at, beaten or teased. The self-esteem and confidence workshop aims to help pupils build a good self-image and identity.

Motivation:
Goal setting is vital for motivation. Interest is an important motivator for students and young people need to be taught how to develop their motivational skills. Motivation is needed at all stages of life. The aim of this workshop is to teach individuals the importance of setting and achieving goals.

Positive Mental Attitude:
Too often young people let negative thoughts overtake their desire to succeed. The challenges of life can become overwhelming rather than seen as opportunities for character development and growth. This workshop focuses on the effects of thoughts, words and actions. It aims to teach the individuals how to think positive and be positive.

Workshop Programs for Teachers/Educators/Parents:
Become runs a series of programmes for educators and parents titled

'Raising Positive Children in a Negative Society.' We deal with channels of communication, trust, respect, and discipline, encouraging the parent/teacher to view life from the perspective of the child. We also talk about what to do when efforts towards the youth seem futile.

Physical activity and healthy eating:

Young people need to be encouraged to do 60 minutes of physical activity at least three times a week. Increasing physical activity holds several benefits such as health, anxiety and self-esteem. We provide a digestible and achievable health and fitness scheme for the pupils. Become brings in specialised experts of specific fields for various topics at no extra cost. We provide professionals who have the right knowledge, experience and expertise.